Unheard Verses: A Collection of Eighty-Sixed Poems

Jennifer Gurney

ISBN: 978-93-6354-546-5

First Edition: 2025
Rs. 200/-

Cyberwit.net
HIG 45 Kaushambi Kunj, Kalindipuram
Allahabad - 211011 (U.P.) India
http://www.cyberwit.net
Tel: +(91) 9415091004
E-mail: info@cyberwit.net

Printed at Repro India Limited.

Dedication

Unheard Verses is dedicated to the editors and publishers who took a chance on me before anyone else did. To Kathleen Trocmet, editor of Scarlet Dragonfly, who published my very first haiku poem and many to follow. To Gretna Wilkinson, founder of The Ravens Perch, who published my very first prose poem and many to follow. To Roberta Beach Jacobson, editor of Five Fleas and founder / past editor of Cold Moon Journal, who published some of my earliest poems and many subsequent poems. To Dr. Agarwal, editor of The TAJ Mahal Review, who published my very first book of poetry, and more to follow. My heartfelt thanks to each one.

clouds paint a picture
of myriad-colored sky
billowy essence

* Submitted to Chrysanthemum 2-3-23, not accepted
* Submitted to Presence 5-13-23, not accepted
* Submitted to Shamrock 6-15-23, not accepted
* Submitted to Inkfish Magazine 4-25-25, not accepted
* Submitted to Hedgerow 5-18-25, not accepted

grief
counting the hours till
darkness comes

* Submitted to First Frost 7-4-24, not accepted
* Submitted to 7th Basho-an International English Haiku Contest 9-15-24, not accepted

quietly you fall
blanketing the night
in silence

* Submitted to Haiku Society of America Haiku Award Contest 7-4-24, not accepted
* Submitted to Heron's Nest 9-14-24, not accepted
* Submitted to Cold Moon Journal 11-2-24, not accepted
* Submitted to Puddock 11-27-24, not accepted
* Submitted to Acorn 1-1-25, not accepted

grateful for
an unexpected plateau
I catch my breath

* Written originally for Postcard Poetry Fest 7-13-24
* Submitted to Five Fleas 8-9-24, not accepted
* Submitted to Failed Haiku 9-11-24, not accepted
* Submitted to Fireflies' Light 9-14-24, not accepted
* Submitted to Haiku Commentary 10-9-24, not accepted
* Submitted to Betty Drevniok Contest 2-7-25, not accepted
* Submitted to Cold Moon Journal 7-1-25, not accepted

I still reach for my phone
to call you with good news –
three years gone

* Submitted to Five Fleas 7-26-24, not accepted
* Submitted to Presence 8-5-24, not accepted
* Submitted to Asahi Haikuist 12-1-24, not accepted

I live with
ghosts of family
past, present, future

* Submitted to Daily Verse 8-6-24, not accepted

gazing westward
inhaling the mountains
sheer uplift

* Submitted to HaikuKatha 8-18-24, not accepted
* Submitted to Haiku Foundation - theme: mountains 3-5-25, not accepted
* Submitted to Acorn 7-2-25, not accepted

gazing skyward
heaven appears
through the clouds

* Submitted to Cicada's Cry 9-14-24, not accepted
* Submitted to Inkfish Magazine 4-25-25, not accepted
* Submitted to Hedgerow 5-18-25, not accepted

how ironic
the darkness of
gaslighting

* Submitted to Five Fleas 11-15-24, not accepted
* Submitted to Puddock 11-27-24, not accepted
* Submitted to Failed Haiku 1-10-25, not accepted
* Submitted to Fresh Out 1-11-25, not accepted
* Submitted to Cold Moon Journal 4-3-25, not accepted
* Submitted to Wales Haiku Journal 6-7-25, not accepted
* Submitted to Acorn 7-2-25, not accepted

some days, all feels brave
the crunch of an apple
the smile of a stranger

* Submitted to Failed Haiku 11-17-24, not accepted
* Submitted to Five Fleas 1-1-25, not accepted

I never know
where I'll be when
a poem descends

* Submitted to Superpresent - Mysteries and Secrets 11-17-24, not accepted
* Submitted to Jackdaw Review 6-11-25, not accepted

a bottle
will forever live on my dresser
your scent

* Submitted to HaikuKatha 11-19-24, not accepted
* Submitted to Five Fleas 12-29-24, not accepted
* Submitted to Fresh Out 4-5-25, not accepted
* Submitted to Cold Moon Journal 7-1-25, not accepted

your visit
all too brief
blue moon

* Submitted to Puddock 11-27-24, not accepted
* Submitted to Acorn 1-1-25, not accepted

Advent
waiting for hope
to descend

* Submitted to Asahi Haikuist 12-1-24, not accepted

when there are no words
my heart turns
to moonlight

* Submitted to Cold Moon Journal 12-1-24, not accepted
* Submitted to Akitsu Quarterly 1-1-25, not accepted
* Submitted to Cold Moon Journal 2-2-25, not accepted
* Submitted to Five Fleas 6-2-25, not accepted
* Submitted to Wales Haiku Journal 6-7-25, not accepted
* Submitted to Acorn 7-2-25, not accepted

dropping in
for a lovely visit
memories

* Submitted to Five Fleas 12-14-24, not accepted
* Submitted to Acorn 1-1-25, not accepted
* Submitted to Fresh Out 4-5-25, not accepted
* Submitted to Cold Moon Journal 7-1-25, not accepted

my life
an unending string of loss
ready for a gain...

* Submitted to Five Fleas 12-14-24, not accepted
* Submitted to Fresh Out 4-5-25, not accepted
* Submitted to Acorn 7-2-25, not accepted

in my
peripheral vision
I still see your smile

* Submitted to Five Fleas 12-14-24, not accepted
* Submitted to Fresh Out 4-5-25, not accepted
* Submitted to Ink in Thirds 7-3-25, not accepted

close in my arms
inhaling your scent
first kiss

* Submitted to Five Fleas 12-29-24, not accepted

stepping into
the fresh, new year
slippers and pjs

* Submitted to Five Fleas 1-1-25, not accepted

my heart burst
into a million pieces
engaged

* Submitted to Five Fleas 1-9-25, not accepted

my heart
spinning around the dancefloor
your news

* Submitted to Five Fleas 1-9-25, not accepted

leaning over the bridge
to catch sky's reflection
I see you in me

* Submitted to Five Fleas 1-11-25, not accepted
* Submitted to Folk Ku - Water Theme 3-20-25, not accepted
* Submitted to Cold Moon Journal 4-3-25, not accepted
* Submitted to Wales Haiku Journal 6-7-25, not accepted
* Submitted to 02 Haiku 7-1-25, not accepted

waking before the sun
or even any tire tracks
in the snow

* Submitted to Five Fleas 1-18-25, not accepted
* Submitted to Tiger Moth Review 3-28-25, not accepted

I will
never understand
misogyny

* Submitted to Five Fleas 3-18-25, not accepted
* Submitted to Helios Sparrow 3-25-25, not accepted
* Submitted to Failed Haiku 5-10-25, not accepted
* Submitted to Femku 5-18-25, not accepted
* Submitted to Modern Haiku 6-15-25, not accepted

a momentary
lapse in judgement
changes everything

* Submitted to Five Fleas 3-18-25, not accepted
* Submitted to Helios Sparrow 3-25-25, not accepted
* Submitted to Failed Haiku 5-10-25, not accepted
* Submitted to Femku 5-18-25, not accepted
* Submitted to Blithe Spirit 6-9-25, not accepted

opening to spring
from winter's cocoon
both sides of me

* Submitted to HaikuKatha 3-20-25, not accepted
* Submitted to Helios Sparrow 4-21-25, not accepted

scattered
in every direction
spring cleaning

* Submitted to Helios Sparrow 3-25-25, not accepted
* Submitted to Five Fleas 4-23-25, not accepted

we shed our coats
as butterflies are born
spring

* Submitted to Poetry Pea video prompt for March 2025 3-25-25, not accepted
* Submitted to LEAF Issue 7, 6-7-25, not accepted

sunlight on water
dancing to its own rhythm
reminds me of you

* Submitted to Helios Sparrow 3-25-25, not accepted
* Submitted to Five Fleas 5-1-25, not accepted
* Submitted to Failed Haiku 5-10-25, not accepted
* Submitted to Flying Fish Haiku Journal 5-18-25, not accepted
* Submitted to HaikuKatha 6-24-25, not accepted

that web of thoughts
that grows around my to do list
procrastination

* Submitted to Five Fleas 3-26-25, not accepted
* Submitted to Wales Haiku Journal 6-7-25, not accepted
* Submitted to Acorn 7-2-25, not accepted

light
through my morning window shade
dancing

* Submitted to Tiger Moth Review 3-28-25, not accepted

in dying
so much living
left behind

* Submitted to Cold Moon Journal 4-3-25, not accepted
* Submitted to Wales Haiku Journal 6-7-25, not accepted
* Submitted to Acorn 7-2-25, not accepted

like cows
I, too
mother for life

* Submitted to Cold Moon Journal 4-3-25, not accepted
* Submitted to Wales Haiku Journal 6-7-25, not accepted
* Submitted to Acorn 7-2-25, not accepted

dreams
underwatered
dying on the vine

* Submitted to Fresh Out 4-5-25, not accepted
* Submitted to Acorn 7-2-25, not accepted

spirits dance
on the periphery of my heart
new memories

* Submitted to Jackdaw 4-7-25, not accepted
* Submitted to Helios Sparrow 4-21-25, not accepted

passage
to the past
open doorways

* Submitted to Five Fleas 4-18-25, not accepted
* Submitted to Hedgerow 5-18-25, not accepted

half the closet blue
half the closet brown
my parents

* Submitted to Five Fleas 4-18-25, not accepted
* Submitted to Failed Haiku 5-10-25, not accepted

day one
you carved a space in my heart
just for you

* Submitted to Five Fleas 4-18-25, not accepted
* Submitted to Cold Moon Journal 5-2-25, not accepted

my favorite
the sky, your eyes, the horizon
color blue

* Submitted to Five Fleas 4-18-25, not accepted
* Submitted to Hedgerow 5-18-25, not accepted

forgetting
the punchline of his joke
he laughs anyway

* Submitted to HaikuKatha 4-20-25, not accepted
* Submitted to Five Fleas 7-3-25, not accepted

basking in the glow
of every single solitary
moment

* Submitted to Helios Sparrow 4-21-25, not accepted

the glow of the flame
warming me from within
morning meditation

* Submitted to Heron's Nest 4-21-25, not accepted

frozen
my heart still wanting
to believe

* Submitted to Heron's Nest 4-21-25, not accepted
* Submitted to Five Fleas 7-3-25, not accepted

Mayo Clinic website
screen blurs through tears
stage four liver cancer

* Submitted to Five Fleas 4-23-25, not accepted

covering the sun
obliterating shadows
clouds

* Submitted to Inkfish Magazine 4-25-25, not accepted
* Submitted to Hedgerow 5-18-25, not accepted

happiness
every time my dad
answers the phone

* Submitted to Cold Moon Journal 5-2-25, not accepted

each day on Facebook
viewing all of your pictures
I travel the world

* Submitted to Haiku Girl Summer 5-26-24, not accepted
* Submitted to Heron's Nest 9-14-24, not accepted
* Submitted to Cold Moon Journal 11-2-24, not accepted
* Submitted to Puddock 11-27-24, not accepted
* Submitted to Tsuri-doro 1-1-25, not accepted
* Submitted to Five Fleas 4-11-25, not accepted

in the gloaming
between life and the final chapter
hope dwells

* Submitted to Five Fleas 5-9-25, not accepted
* Submitted to Failed Haiku 5-10-25, not accepted
* Submitted to Under the Basho 5-18-25, not accepted
* Submitted to Modern Haiku 6-15-25, not accepted
* Submitted to Acorn 7-2-25, not accepted

I fall to pieces
Mother's Day
without you

* Submitted to The Cicada's Cry 5-10-25, not accepted

the sky's reflection
on the surface of your calm
blue twins

* Submitted to HaikuKatha 5-10-25, not accepted

bedtime ritual
putting the house to sleep
then me

* Submitted to Fresh Out 5-11-25, not accepted
* Submitted to Under the Basho 5-18-25, not accepted

all that remains
sun against bare branches
silhouette shadow

* Submitted to Fresh Out 5-11-25, not accepted
* Submitted to Hedgerow 5-18-25, not accepted

distance shrinks
with every single
memory

* Submitted to Five Fleas 5-18-25, not accepted

what I wouldn't give
to open my mailbox
to a postcard from you...

* Submitted to Five Fleas 5-18-25, not accepted

withered lilacs
in a now-dry jar
on their way to the bin

* Submitted to HaikuKatha 5-18-25, not accepted

I slow blink to you
in your own sweet time
you slow blink back to me

* Submitted to Hedgerow 5-18-25, not accepted

windows open
lilac-scented air wafts in
from another life

* Submitted to Hedgerow 5-18-25, not accepted

there was
nothing quite like
your-hand-in-mine calm

* Submitted to Hedgerow 5-18-25, not accepted

there is a tether
between my heart below
and the clouds above

* Submitted to HaikuKatha 6-1-24, not accepted
* Submitted to Presence 8-5-24, not accepted
* Submitted to Inkfish Magazine 4-25-25, not accepted
* Submitted to Hedgerow 5-18-25, not accepted

every time
I fry an egg
I think of you

* Submitted to Five Fleas 6-2-25, not accepted

hearing your voice
for perhaps the last time
each call, now

* Submitted to Five Fleas 6-3-25, not accepted

day warming
the magic of dew-covered
leaves unfurling

* Submitted to Wales Haiku Journal 6-7-25, not accepted
* Submitted to Acorn 7-2-25, not accepted

in the shade of your memory
I rest from this
wilting grief

* Submitted to HaikuKatha 6-7-25, not accepted

a candle snuffed too early
lingering trail of smoke
memories of your light

* Submitted to HaikuKatha 6-7-25, not accepted

deadheading the roses
a lone dragonfly alights
stealing the nectar from the day

* Submitted to Wales Haiku Journal 6-7-25, not accepted
* Submitted to Acorn 7-2-25, not accepted

on the surface
deep
still calm

* Submitted to Wales Haiku Journal 6-7-25, not accepted
* Submitted to Acorn 7-2-25, not accepted

summer rain evening's lullaby watering my arid heart

* Submitted to HaikuKatha 6-7-25, not accepted

shading myself
from the world
new grief

* Submitted to HaikuKatha 6-8-25, not accepted

between
darkness and dawn
memories lighten

* Submitted to HaikuKatha 6-8-25, not accepted

skirting
the busy June wedding season
5-25-25

* Submitted to Five Fleas 6-8-25, not accepted

first night
without you on earth
interminable
an eternity
till sun’s rise

* Submitted to HaikuKatha 6-8-25, not accepted

rain muddies my path to you sucking my steps from me

* Submitted to HaikuKatha 6-8-25, not accepted

though the window
roses bloom, bursting with life
your voice on the phone brings me his death

* Submitted to HaikuKatha 6-13-25, not accepted

Father's Day
on the lake
your ashes

* Submitted to Five Fleas 6-13-25, not accepted
* Submitted to Modern Haiku 6-15-25, not accepted
* Submitted to Acorn 7-2-25, not accepted

steady stream
day and night
memories

* Submitted to Modern Haiku 6-15-25, not accepted
* Submitted to Acorn 7-2-25, not accepted

if only...
six letters, two words, three dots
such power

* Submitted to Modern Haiku 6-15-25, not accepted
* Submitted to Acorn 7-2-25, not accepted

sunrise
one more day
with you in it

* Submitted to Modern Haiku 6-15-25, not accepted
* Submitted to Acorn 7-2-25, not accepted

every heart
beats in symmetry
together, apart

* Submitted to Modern Haiku 6-15-25, not accepted
* Submitted to Acorn 7-2-25, not accepted

first plunge
icy cold Lake Michigan
liquid summer bliss

* Submitted to Haiku Shack Issue 3 - theme: what brings you joy 6-15-25, not accepted

meeting my granddaughter
for the very first time
Joy

* Submitted to Haiku Shack Issue 3 - theme: what brings you joy
6-15-25, not accepted

under the stars
dancing like no one is watching
rhythm of joy

* Submitted to Haiku Shack Issue 3 - theme: what brings you joy 6-15-25, not accepted

even after
the rose's bloom fades
potpourri

* Submitted to HaikuKatha 6-15-25, not accepted

summer
suspended on the tightrope of disbelief
fresh grief

* Submitted to Five Fleas 6-18-25, not accepted
* Submitted to Ink in Thirds 7-3-25, not accepted

worst nightmare
every day
present tense

* Submitted to Nick Virgilio Haiku in Action - Our Wildest Dreams 6-18-25, not accepted
* Submitted to Five Fleas 7-3-25, not accepted

memories
reflected
summer mirror

* Submitted to Five Fleas 6-18-25, not accepted

summer
reflected in hose water
sidewalk mirror

* Submitted to HaikuKatha 6-18-25, not accepted

all floppy feet and water spray
yet, uncanny in its gracefulness
pelican landing

* Submitted to HaikuKatha 6-21-25, not accepted

even
before the first drop falls
I smell rain

* Submitted to HaikuKatha 6-24-25, not accepted

air full of
the coming storm
electricity

* Submitted to Five Fleas 6-25-25, not accepted

counting the days
till sand beneath my toes
Michigan

* Submitted to Five Fleas 6-25-25, not accepted

littering the beach
ocean's pixie dust
shells

* Submitted to Five Fleas 6-25-25, not accepted

waves of calm
wash over my shore
pulling grief away with the tide

* Submitted to Five Fleas 6-25-25, not accepted

even after centuries
love ingrained can start to fade
petroglyph

* Submitted to HaikuKatha 6-28-25, not accepted

mourning dove on my roof
singing its lament
in harmony with my soul

* Submitted to Five Fleas 6-29-25, not accepted
* Submitted to Ink in Thirds 7-3-25, not accepted

every grain of sand
every wave and sunset
my favorite beach read

* Submitted to Five Fleas 6-29-25, not accepted

a lake full of birds
I only have eyes for
you

* Submitted to Five Fleas 6-29-25, not accepted

every morning
every evening
turn

* Submitted to Five Fleas 6-29-25, not accepted

diaphanous clouds
drifting against an azure sky
painting day's canvas

* Submitted to Cold Moon Journal 7-1-24, not accepted
* Submitted to Inkfish Magazine 4-25-25, not accepted
* Submitted to Hedgerow 5-18-25, not accepted

gentle tendrils
smoke in the morning air
bonfire's ghost

* Submitted to Cold Moon Journal 7-1-25, not accepted

you are my wildfire
all that heat and spark
and kindling

* Submitted to Cold Moon Journal 7-1-25, not accepted

I long to be lifted
up and away from this heavy, dark grief
I watch the egret, soaring, with envy

* Submitted to Acorn 7-2-25, not accepted

for a moment
I can taste the me who was alive
before you died

* Submitted to Acorn 7-2-25, not accepted

lying on my lap
sinking into me with love
you ground me

* Submitted to Acorn 7-2-25, not accepted

sun on bare skin
energizes me onward
solar power

* Submitted to Fresh Out 7-2-25, not accepted

my favorite sculptor
carving images from paint on canvas
Van Gogh

* Submitted to Five Fleas 7-3-25, not accepted

when all my roses
bloom at once
plethora of petals

* Submitted to Five Fleas 7-3-25, not accepted

east in the time zone
home in Michigan
light longer later

* Submitted to Five Fleas 7-17-25, not accepted

my glass
sweating as much as me
iced tea

* Submitted to Five Fleas 7-17-25, not accepted

my drink of choice
front porch happy hour
iced tea

* Submitted to Five Fleas 7-17-25, not accepted

in between visits
I blink
so tall!

* Submitted to Five Fleas 7-17-25, not accepted

between my toes
the sweet tickle
grass

* Submitted to Five Fleas 7-17-25, not accepted

the trees
all taller
than I remember

* Submitted to Five Fleas 7-17-25, not accepted

my friend's garden
beaucolic morning
Michigan summer

* Submitted to Five Fleas 7-17-25, not accepted

moon rise
along with my heart
full

* Submitted to Five Fleas 7-17-25, not accepted

your eyes
a mirror of
love

* Submitted to Five Fleas 7-17-25, not accepted

your love
hydration for
my heart

* Submitted to Five Fleas 7-17-25, not accepted

www.ingramcontent.com/pod-product-compliance
Ingram Content Group UK Ltd.
Pitfield, Milton Keynes, MK11 3LW, UK
UKHW041314190726
13845UKWH00025B/268

9 789363 545465